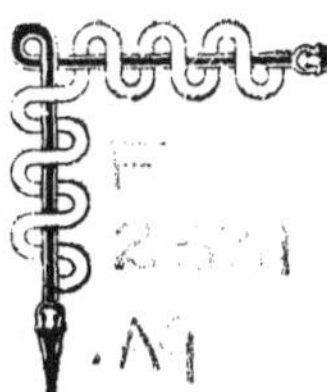

MEMOIR

JUSTIFICATORY OF THE CONDUCT

OF

THE GOVERNMENT OF VENEZUELA

ON THE

ISLA DE AVES QUESTION,

PRESENTED

TO HIS EXCELLENCY THE SECRETARY OF STATE
OF THE UNITED STATES.

BY THE ENVOY EXTRAORDINARY AND MINISTER PLENIPOTENTIARY
OF VENEZUELA,

DOCTOR MARIANO DE BRICEÑO.

WASHINGTON CITY,
1858.

F. H. SAGE, PRINTER.

MEMOIR

JUSTIFICATORY OF THE CONDUCT

OF

THE GOVERNMENT OF VENEZUELA

ON THE

ISLA DE AVES QUESTION,

PRESENTED

TO HIS EXCELLENCY THE SECRETARY OF STATE

OF THE UNITED STATES,

BY THE ENVOY EXTRAORDINARY AND MINISTER PLENIPOTENTIARY

OF VENEZUELA,

DOCTOR MARIANO DE BRICEÑO.

WASHINGTON CITY,

1858.

F. H. SAGE, PRINTER.

STATEMENTS.

1854, June.—About the middle of the year, 1854, two mercantile firms of Boston, Lang & Delano, and Sampson, Tappan & Shelton, despatched vessels for the purpose of discovering guano on desert islands lying in the Carribean sea, and taking possession thereof. The vessels, which sailed clandestinely from Boston on the expedition, were the "John R. Don" and "M. H. Comery," the former belonging to Shelton & Co., and the latter to Lang & Delano. The fact of their clandestine departure from Boston is clearly proven by the books of the custom-house at that port. Other vessels sailed afterwards during the same year from various ports of the United States for Isla de Aves.

1854, July.—James Wheeler, agent of Lang & Delano, invaded Isla de Aves. A few hours afterwards, William P. Gibbs, as the agent of Shelton & Co., also arrived there. The island is situated in 15° 45′ north latitude, and 63° 35′ west longitude from Greenwich, W. ¼ - S.E. from the French island of Gaudaloupe. Its dimensions are about 700 yards in length, by 125 in breadth, and 12 in height. It is liable to be overflown by the sea during storms—waterless and uninhabited. The filibusters immediately employed themselves in the extraction of the guano they found there, within the limits they prescribed for their respective operations.

1854, December 12.—The Government of Venezuela, on being informed of the invasion of the island, despatched thither a national armed schooner, under the command of Colonel Diaz, which arrived at its destination on the evening of the above date. He met there three vessels at anchor, ready to take cargoes of guano on board, one of 800 tons, and another of 600 tons. The crew of the Venezuelan armed schooner consisted of 27 men; her armament of 27 muskets, one four-pounder, with a suitable quantity of munitions of war. The filibusters at Isla de Aves were 80 in number, armed with 50 pair of pistols carrying ounce balls, about 40 muskets, boarding pikes and hatchets, two 6 and 8-pounders with a proportionate quantity of balls, and about two quintals of powder.

1854, December 13.—Colonel Diaz, being in the peaceful occupation of the island, ascertained from the said filibusters that they were engaged in clandestinely exporting the guano from Isla de Aves, and other uninhabited islands belonging to Venezuela.

1854, December 13.—At the request of the filibusters, Colonel Diaz, as commissioner of Venezuela, gives permission at the island for three American vessels to complete their cargoes without molestation from any of the West India cruisers. By this permit, which was signed by Colonel Diaz and the two agents, Nathan P. Gibbs for Shelton & Co., and Charles H. Lang for Lang & Delano, the filibusters were allowed not only to complete the loading of the three vessels with the guano, but to continue the further exportation thereof until the arrival of the legitimate contractors of the Venezuelan Government, on the following conditions, viz: 1st, that the latter should approve thereof; 2d, that the two Boston agents should furnish certain supplies required by the Venezuelan garrison; and 3d, that they should place the whole of their armaments under the orders of the authority of Venezuela and under its flag; all which was accordingly done, to the satisfaction of all the parties, except the Government at Caracas, which disavowed the transaction.

1854, DECEMBER 21.—The Government of Venezuela at Caracas, makes a concession for fifteen years to Mr. Wallace, a citizen of the United States, of all the guano on Isla de Aves and of the other islands of the Republic, in consideration of certain cash payments which the contractor obligated himself to make by means of drafts which he drew in favor of the Government.

1854, DECEMBER 30.—By order of the agent of the Venezuelan Government, the filibusters peaceably left Isla de Aves laden with all the guano they had shipped, without avowing the least intention of making the international claim which they afterwards interposed.

1855, JANUARY 15.—Shelton and associates make application to the Government of the United States, soliciting its intervention to be indemnified by Venezuela, not only for the losses they alleged to have suffered by reason of their expulsion, but likewise for the ulterior profits they expected to realize from the further exportation of the guano.

1855, MARCH.—Mr. Eames, Minister Resident of the United States in Caracas, obtains, privately, the copy of a document filed in the office of the Secretary of State of Venezuela, in which the agents of Shelton and his associates acknowledged, when on the island, the sovereignty of Venezuela over the same. Mr. Eames, who was not aware of the existence of such a document, brings it to the knowledge of his government, and thereby retards the formal presentation of the claim until the time hereinafter mentioned.

1855, APRIL 30.—Mr. Wallace assigns his contract to a mercantile firm, composed of American citizens, under the title of the "Guano Company of Philadelphia," which obtained an act of incorporation from the Legislature of Pennsylvania of the above date.

1855, MAY 22.—The drafts having been protested for non-acceptance, the Wallace contract was annulled by the Government of Venezuela.

1855, JUNE AND AUGUST.—In these months Shelton & Co. take the declarations of their agents, and other persons, with the object of sustaining their projected reclamation on account of their having been expelled from Isla de Aves.

1855, July 28.—Decree of the President of Venezuela, opening to foreign commerce the exportation of guano from Isla de Aves, and the other islands of the Republic.

1855, AUGUST.—In this month the American filibusters returned to export guano clandestinely from the desert islands on the coast of Venezuela. During this and the following months were detected at Los Monjes, the American bark "Corwin;" at the Island of Pié, the American schooner "White Swan;" and at Los Hermanos another American schooner that left eighty bags of guano in its flight.

1855, SEPTEMBER 2.—The American Guano Company of Philadelphia, on being apprised of the cancelling of the Wallace contract, solicits the protection of the Government of the United States, and obtains it, to compel Venezuela to sustain them as the assignees of the Wallace contract; John Pickrell was in consequence despatched as its agent in the American schooner White Swan, which arrived at Isla de Aves on the above mentioned date. As was naturally to be expected, she was prohibited from loading with guano; he then entered a protest, making the actual costs amount to $50,000, and the contingent damages to $500,000.

1855, SEPTEMBER.—Arrival of Pickrell at Caracas. Sustained by the Legation of the United States, he demands the restoration of the Wallace contract, the principal object of which was the working of the guano on Isla de Aves.

1855, SEPTEMBER 24.—Date of the *Memorandum* of the conference with the President of Venezuela, signed by Mr. Eames, Minister Resident of the United States in Caracas, which shows, 1st, the importance attached by the American Legation to the Pickrell claim; 2d the first *written mention of the other claim of Shelton*, which he *contemplated* establishing by reason of the disposession of American citizens at Isla de Aves ; and 3d, of Mr. Eames declining the discussion of the two conflicting claims at the same time.

1855, SEPTEMBER 29.—The Government of Venezuela, out of its regard for the public peace, renews in favor of the Philadelphia Company the Wallace contract, with certain modifications in regard to the price of the guano to be exported.

1856, MARCH.—Netherland vessels of war arrive at La Guayra with an *ultimatum*, demanding the recognition of the Dutch right to Isla de Aves, and the withdrawal of troops stationed there. Mr. Eames, on being made officially informed, at his own request, of the matter, addressed a note on the 8th of March to the Secretary of Foreign Relations of Venezuela, opposing the Dutch demand for the surrender of the island, partly on account of the claim which it was *his intention to make* in regard to that island in favor of the Americans who had first discovered guano thereon, and also in behalf of the *rights conferred on Pickrell in respect thereto.*

1856, APRIL AND MAY.—During these months Shelton & Company take the last extra-judicial declarations, before a Notary in New York, to invalidate the permit of 13th December.

1856, DECEMBER 20.—The Minister of the United States addresses the Government of Venezuela, *his first official note*, holding it responsible for the occupation of Isla de Aves, and demanding indemnity in favor of the citizens of the United States expelled therefrom, without stating who they were.

1857, FEBRUARY 27.—The Government of Venezuela repels the claim in a judicious note.

1857, MARCH 31.—Mr. Eames insists in an official communication notable for its length.

1857, APRIL.—The President of Venezuela submits the matter to the consideration of the Government Council.

1857, MAY.—The Government Council orders that proof be taken to refute the assertion of Shelton that his agent had signed the permit of December 13, by means of fraud and violence.

1857, MAY 29.—The Legation of the United States addresses a note to the Government of Venezuela, charging it with undue delay in acknowledging the justice of the indemnity demanded, and alleging that such delay was calculated to place in *imminent* peril the friendly relations between the two countries!

1857, JUNE.—The proof ordered by the Government Council was completed. Mr. Eames was invited to be present at the taking of the testimony, but declined attending.

1857, JUNE 11.—Mr. Eames having the permission of his government to return to the United States, makes a formal demand for his passports as the result of the pending question.

1857, JUNE 12.—The Government of Venezuela sends Mr. Eames his passports, informing him that the substantiation of the pending claim was not yet concluded. It added, that both cabinets would come to a direct understanding on the subject in the event of there being no minister of the United States in Caracas.

1857, August 5.—Convention between Venezuela and Holland, submitting the question of Isla de Aves to arbitration.

1857, October.—Mr. Eames returns to Caracas. The Government of Venezuela victoriously refutes the claim in a note of the 31st of same month, remits the negotiation to Washington, and sends a special Minister Plenipotentiary to this capital.

ARGUMENT.

Such are the facts connected with the Isla de Aves question, all of which are most clearly proved by official acts.

Among these facts there stands one which constitutes the actual *state of the controversy* now pending between Venezuela and the United States, namely:

The prohibition to export guano from Isla de Aves, imposed by Venezuela on American citizens, who occupied it in December, 1854.

The two contending parties agree upon this point, but differ in its qualification. The Government of the United States looks upon it as an act of violent encroachment upon rightful property. Venezuela denies this qualification. It is therefore a case in which rhetoric and law have jointly, and from the most remote antiquity, consecrated the principle that:

"It lies upon the accuser to prove what the other denies. In this case the state of the cause is taken from the indictment."

Otherwise the advantages of the aggressor would become far greater. Filibusters, for instance, could take possession of any uninhabited island, any desert territory never trodden by human foot, of which there is so much in Spanish America. This island or territory has an owner; but filibusters consider it as a derelict domain. They invade and establish dominion over it. The rightful possessor thereof repels the aggressor, who, in his turn, assumes the character of the party aggrieved, and with that arrogance which always accompanies bold injustice, exclaims:—"This island, this territory is not yours; whatever you may aver to the contrary, I disregard; you must produce the proofs, for the simple reason that I choose to constitute myself both judge and party in this matter." Common sense suffices to show how untenable such a supposition would be.

If the claimants, the Secretary of State, Mr. Marcy, and the Minister Resident at Caracas, Mr. Eames, have alleged that the proof on the question appertains to Venezuela, it is because they have *supposed as unquestionable* the identical matter in controversy, that is to say, "that Isla de Aves, up to July 1854, had no owner, for being uninhabitable, it was never taken possession of by any government." So true it is that such a proposition has only proceeded from mere supposition, that Mr. Marcy, without sufficient knowledge of the case, and on the claim being presented to his Department, decides upon the question in January 24, 1855, in these terms:—

"Aves Islands have been known probably more than three hundred years, but have ever been regarded uninhabitable and valueless. No nation has deemed them of sufficient importance to be *reduced* to possession. *As we understand* the case, Aves Islands were not embraced within the sovereignty of any power, but were derelict." [*Official note from Mr. Marcy to Mr. Eames. Documents respecting the Aves Islands referred to the Committee of Foreign Relations of the Senate. January* 20, 1857.]

It would have been natural to expect that Mr. Marcy, in view alone of the unquestionable fact of the discovery of Isla de Aves three centuries ago, had deduced and recognized its occupation by some government, and abstained from officially countenancing the claim introduced by Shelton and his associates. He would thus have respected the principle in virtue of which, Spain, about the year 1679, expelled from the desert islands of Providence those Englishmen who had unlawfully occupied it; the same principle which the United States invoked in favor of the Oregon question with Great Britain, and the very identical principle which Mr. Dobbin, a colleague of Mr. Marcy during Mr. Pierce's administration, left untouched in his instructions of October 20th, 1855, which, in relation to an uninhabited island in the Pacific Ocean, said to have been discovered by an American citizen, he, Mr. Dobbin, gave to Commodore Mervine, directing him to abstain from occupying it, and to confine himself to acquiring information, should he find that island had been discovered by other people.

Notwithstanding such valuable precedents, Mr. Marcy overlooked the fact of previous discovery when the subject of Isla de Aves was brought up; and not only did he overlook that fact, but even allowed himself to suppose that it remained abandoned and without an owner, at the time of transmitting the claim of Shelton and his associates to the United States Legation at Caracas.

Mr. Eames replies however: " that the Island had always been considered *by all governments as derelict, is perhaps not quite so certain,*" and he proved it by the pretensions which Holland was about interposing thereto. (*Note from Mr. Eames to Mr. Marcy, Caracas, April 26th,* 1855—*Document aforesaid.*)

But afterwards, this doubt was removed from the mind of Mr. Eames, establishing, as unquestionable a controvertible spoliation, in order to deduce therefrom the liability of Venezuela, notwithstanding the additional strong reasons he had for such doubt, arising out of the *formal* claim presented by Holland.

From the above premises, it clearly results that Venezu la is not bound to furnish the proofs. Nevertheless she has already adduced them, because she has justice on her side, and loses nothing thereby.

The complete justification of Venezuela results from the following propositions, all of which are set forth in the note of the Hon. Jacinto Gutierrez, Secretary of Foreign Affairs, dated October 31st, 1857, to which reference is made in this Memoir, the object of which is to furnish a condensed statement of the arguments in said document, and to present some additional ones of importance.

1st. Isla de Aves was discovered and taken possession of by Spain.

2d. Isla de Aves was incorporated under the Captain Generalship of Venezuela at the time of her emancipation from Spain, and is therefore at the present day an integral portion of the Republic of Venezuela.

3d. Even if Isla de Aves did not belong to the Republic of Venezuela, it could not be regarded as derelict in July 1854, since Holland still persists is asserting her claim, however unjustly, to the ownership thereof.

4th. Supposing that Isla de Aves was derelict in July, 1854, which is the ground taken by the claimants, Venezuela as a nation should, in competition with private citizens, be considered the rightful occupant, accordiug to international law.

5th. The Government of the United States itself recognized the sovereignty of Venezuela over Isla de Aves, when in September 1855, it interposed an energetic demand in favor of the Pickrell claim.

6th. Venezuela has in no manner whatsoever incurred any responsibility towards the United States by her prohibition to export guano from Isla de Aves, imposed on American citizens who in 1854 had occupied it.

PROPOSITION FIRST.

Isla de Aves was the property of Spain—The history of discoveries shows that Spanish navigators visited all that group called the Windward islands, extending from St. Domingo in a semicircular direction to the coast of Guyana in Venezuela, as well as all others of the littoral of that Republic. The very name of Isla de Aves plainly shows the nation which discovered it in the ocean.

The Compilation of Indies contains a law prescribing the formalities by which Spanish discoverers were to be governed in taking possession of territories in America. It runs thus: " We command chiefs, captains, and any other persons who may discover any island or mainland, on landing thereon, *to take possession thereof in our name*, performing such acts as may be deemed expedient, and authenticating the same in a public form and manner to serve as testimony. (*Law 11th, tit 2d book 4th of Compilation of Indies.*)

In 1526 all the Windward islands, among which Isla de Aves is included, and those on the coast of Terra Firme, were comprised, together with the dependency of Venezuela, in the jurisdiction of the Audiencia of St. Domingo. (*See law 2d tit 15th book 11th Compilation of Indies.*)

In said compilation we read the regulations of subsequent date which the Spanish Government dictated for the navigation and commerce of the Windward islands. They are acts of jurisdiction, showing indubitably that Spain did possess Isla de Aves until the early part of this century, when it became the property of Venezuela, as will be seen in the sequel.

It is therefore evident, in respect to an uninhabitable island, that the possession in dispute could not have been material, but as it is termed in law, *civil, in habitu*, which consists in holding the thing habitually or mentally, just such a possession as the various nations of Europe and America, and even Venezuela, still maintain of other unhabitable islands in the Carribean Sea, Los Monjes, Los Hermanos, &c , figuring among them.

By no possible logical argumentation can it be asserted that Spain, as it pleased Mr. Marcy to suppose, ever renounced the right of possession during the period of her sway, on the plea of Isla de Aves being uninhabitable or worthless at that time. If these conditions were necessary for the retaining of possession, no nation could rest secure in relation to such islands as are unsusceptible of material occupation. This is the reason why the law of nations has consecrated the doctrine—" that when there are in any State, desert and uncultivated places, no one is authorized to take possession thereof without the consent of the Sovereign. Although not in actual use of such places, he is notwithstanding the possessor, it is his interest to preserve them, and he is not accountable to any person for the manner in which he makes use of the property."

Moreover, the same Compilation of Indies precludes all doubt upon this point, granting there was any. The Emperor Charles V. and his successors, by various express Royal acts, on declaring themselves lords of the West Indian *Islands* and Continents already discovered and in the way of discovery, dictated the following—" And considering the faithfulness of our subjects, and the hardships endured by the discoverers and settlers in the discovering and settling thereof, we do, in order to their greater certainty of, and confidence in those lands always remaining united to our Royal Crown, promise and pledge our Faith and Royal word for us and the Kings, our successors, never to alienate nor separate them, neither their cities nor towns for any cause or reason, or in favor of any person; and if we, or our successors should make any donation or transfer in defiance of the above, the same to stand null, and so we declare it. (*Law 1st tit 1st book 3d Compilation of Indies still in force.*)

If such strong foundations were lost sight of by a distinguished statesman, which is excusable in the hasty proceedings for the substantiation of a claim, it is to be hoped they will bring irresistible conviction to the just administration now ruling in the United States, where the question must be finally decided.

It then appears as absolutely untenable that Spain has ever spontaneously and tacitly renounced the possession of, or has she alienated Isla de Aves, without those previous express acts in virtue of which she has from imperious political circumstances, given up some of her American colonies.

It has already been proved that Spain did possess Isla de Aves up to the time when it became the property of the Venezuelan nation, for the reasons manifested in the following—

PROPOSITION SECOND.

Isla de Aves the property of Venezuela as succeeding to the rights of Spain. With pain indeed does Venezuela disinter from dusty archives her title of property over Isla de Aves, in order to free herself from the indemnity demanded by filibusterism repelled from a territory where the rightful owner has but exercised acts of sovereignty, for which no accountability is incurred if better title is not produced.

The representative of the United States at Caracas, Mr. Eames, in an official note of 31st March 1856, has acknowledged the following :

" All of the territory of these Continental Governments formed orginally part of the jurisdiction of the Government of St. Domingo and were successively excinded out of it. But besides that vast continental territory, the Government of St. Domingo as appears in the " Leyes de Indias," published at Madrid in 1786, lib. 11 tit 15. comprehended also all the *Windward islands*, as we have seen the Aves in question is found, and this group of islands was *never* taken out of the jurisdiction by Spain, or assigned to the jurisdiction of any of her Continental Governments, *and least of all to Venezuela*, which was at first a dependency of the Vice Royalty of New Granada, and so continued till 1751."

It is therefore acknowledged that Isla de Aves was never taken out of the jurisdiction of Spain. Although the adverb *never* is a surplus word, for the reason further on to be explained, it is important however to remark that Mr. Eames agrees to Isla de Aves having never been abandoned, and consequently he has thus left the claim without even the ground upon which he thought to be able to establish it. Nor is this the only contradiction incurred by Mr. Eames; but they cannot be pointed out, as it is not the purpose of this Memoir to enter into any other expositions than such as directly and substantially relate to the question.

Mr. Eames, we have seen, agrees that Isla de Aves was owned by Spain, but does not admit her having been assigned to the Captain Generalship of Venezuela. The contrary is proved in this manner.

In 1526, all the Windward islands (Aves included) and those of Costa Firme, were assigned to the district of the Audiencia de Santo Domingo. (*L.* 2 *tit* 15 *lib* 11 *Comp. Ind. already mentioned.*)

In 1751, the Captain Generalship of Caracas, or Venezuela, was established, and here is the authentic document showing how the Windward islands (Aves included) were assigned to the Audiencia of Caracas. Mr. Eames has overlooked or been ignorant of such an official act.

The royal decree, dated June 13, 1786, creating the Audiencia of Caracas, runs as follows :

" . . . . In order to avoid the prejudices which are originated to the inhabitants of the province of Maracaybo, also to that of Cumana, Guayana, Margarita, and

Trinidad (a Windward island,) comprised in the Captain-Generalship of Caracas, from having to recur for appeal in their affairs to the Pretorial Audiencia of St. Domingo; the King hath resolved to create another one in Caracas, composed, for the present, of one senior judge, three auditors, and one fiscal, leaving an equal number of judges in that of St. Domingo, and limiting their district to that of the Spanish portion of that island, Cuba and Puerto Rico, to which end His Majesty doth from henceforth appoint such judges as will serve in both islands."

If, therefore, it is unquestionable that in 1786 the Windward islands—Aves included—were attached to the Audiencia of St. Domingo, it should also be clear of all doubt, that since the 13th of June of the same year they were *excluded* from said Audiencia, to be assigned to that of Caracas.

The royal decree of 1786—the right of Venezuela to Isla de Aves—stands of irresistible conviction, from the peculiar circumstance that this islet is found among a group of important islands, named altogether the Windward islands. Without this circumstance, it had been impossible to fix the series of their jurisdictional allottings.

If an analogous question should in future arise in relation to the desert islands in the littoral of Venezuela, the inquiry would prove more difficult, because not being embraced within a common important denomination, their trifling value has been the cause that no mention of them has been made in any law of territorial decision, either in Columbia or Venezuela; so that, officially, it is not known to which province of the Republic they belong. However, no one doubts by what nation they are possessed.

But it will be said that those islands are contiguous to the littoral of Venezuela, and that the one in question is so far off, that Colonel Codazzi omitted assigning it to the Republic in those maps which he got up by order of the government.

When the property of anything is proved by legal instruments, it matters not how far it is situated. If it is true, as is doubtless the fact, that Isla de Aves was incorporated into the Captain-Generalship of Caracas, the question is then at an end.

The legitimacy of Venezuela's right is corroborated by the fact that the only nation which, by reason of proximity, could have claimed Isla de Aves, is France, by alleging that on the invasion of Guadaloupe in 1635, she also *meant* to take possession of it—and yet France has not undertaken such a pretension—which, let it be said in passing, would be less strange than that of the American citizens, who ground it upon the untenable assertion of the abandonment of the islet in question.

The omission of Colonel Codazzi is no proof at all. True it is, that his labors were the result of the special commission entrusted to him by the legislative power, who remunerated his services in an appropriate manner.

Howbeit, it does not follow that his work is strictly official, and much less that it has been approved of as every way perfect and exact by the Government of Venezuela.

It would indeed be exceedingly strange to lay aside that documental proof which clears off the pending controversy, in order to make it dependent upon the insignificant and unforeseen accident of the imperceptible point of an islet, at that time worthless in all respects, being omitted in some maps.

We have it then that Isla de Aves, being included in the Captain-Generalship of Venezuela at the time of the emancipation from Spain, became an integral part of Colombia. This Republic being dissolved in 1830, Venezuela constituted herself into an independent nation, comprising all the territory of the aforesaid Captain-Generalship. It was so declared by her fundamental constitution and in the treaty of peace and recognition between Venezuela and H. C. M., who, in article 2d, "recognizes the Republic of Venezuela as a free, sovereign and independent nation, composed of the provinces and territories expressed in her constitution and other subsequent laws, and also of any other territories or *islands* to which she may be entitled."

PROPOSITION THIRD.

ISLA DE AVES NEVER ABANDONED, DERELICT.—In order to overthrow the specious grounds of the claim in all the branches of its argumentation, let it be supposed for a moment that Venezuela did not succeed Spain in her rights over Isla de Aves. The conclusion that the islet was not under possession in July, 1854, is not thus the more logical nor legitimate.

Hence, it is not possible to imagine there is in the Carribean Sea—already so well known and explored—a foot of land unoccupied by some nation.

Isla de Aves then, if not the property of Venezuela, should belong to Spain, as has been shown in proposition first. But Spain has not claimed Isla de Aves as her own, nor has France, nor England claimed it as annexed to any of their respective colonies. Does it follow, then, that it stood abandoned at the time mentioned? No; because, supposing that to be the case, there would yet be an opening for the pretensions of Holland with regard to the island.

It would not be consistent with the wisdom which distinguishes the Government of the United States in its administration, nor with the principles of justice which guide its conduct, independent of the indestructible proofs of rightful property presented by Venezuela, to give more importance to the mere allegations of two or three American citizens, who, for the sake of speculation, maintain the abandonment of Isla de Aves, than to the assertion of two sovereign nations, who, although differing about the property, both agree upon the substantial point that Isla de Aves has never been derelict.

PROPOSITION FOURTH.

ISLA DE AVES DERELICT, VENEZUELA THE FIRST OCCUPANT.—In order to carry the gracious concessions to their ultimate expression, let it be supposed that Isla de Aves were absolutely abandoned—in a condition to receive primary occupation.

Even on this false supposition, the citizens of the United States who made their way into Isla de Aves, in 1854, could not be deemed the proprietors of said island.

The United States Legation has in no manner whatever demanded the island for the nation. She has never maintained that it is their property—the reason why she has not insisted upon its evacuation and delivery. She solely and exclusively demands pecuniary indemnification. What title does she invoke? Merely previous occupation by American citizens.

Well, then, on the supposition assumed, it is undeniable that the occupation by Venezuela should prevail against that of the American citizens, and should also produce the legal effects of which the occupation by private individuals is not susceptible, looked upon by international law as rash and preposterous, the moment one man presumes alone to arrogate to himself an exclusive right over some territory, in order to constitute himself into a monarch without subjects.

The parties claiming have given proofs that they are conscious of the injury done to their pretensions by that well received doctrine, when they endeavor to demonstrate the contrary in their "Memoranda of the case for the State Department," laying down principles at variance with the rights acquired by nations, and forcing the interpretation of those already recognized in their enlightened practice; but in the midst of the false doctrine diffused in their document, there always shines through the true one, as, for instance, in the following passage;

"Discovery by private citizens vests rights in the United States. It is entirely immaterial whether such discoverer is *a private citizen* or *subject*, or a commissioned officer of a State. The same rights in either case vest in the State to which he belongs. ☞ Vattel only refers to discoveries furnished with a commission from their sovereign; and this was the British argument in the Oregon case." ☜

But the most convincing proof that the claimants did not trust to the force of their demonstrations, is furnished by the bill (*ad hoc*) which they submitted to the consideration of Congress with the object of declaring the rights "of American citizens who may discover and occupy derelict guano islands, &c."

The following are presented as foundations:

"WHEREAS, The rights of the first discoverer of any island, key or rock not appertaining to any State by contiguity, unless followed and perfected by continued possession and actual occupation thereof, becomes extinguished, and therefrom or upon the abandonment of such possession, subsequent discoverers may take possession of and occupy such derelict island:

"AND WHEREAS, also, such subsequent, discovery, possession and occupation, whether by a commissioned officer of the United States *or by a citizen thereof not in the public service, doth cause to inure to and vest in the Federal Government of the United States the plenary right of sovereignty or eminent domain over and to the same, unless expressly declined by the Executive or the Congress of the United States:*

"AND WHEREAS, *also, said discovery and possession and occupation by such citizen vest in such citizen the right to possess such island, key or rock, and exercise the ownership thereof and of all that may be found thereon, exclusively against all States and persons whatsoever, except the Government of the United States aforesaid,* which has full power to restrain or regulate such exercise, and to limit such exercise by law:

"AND WHEREAS, to allow commissioned officers or others in the public service of the United States, to acquire such individual rights by such discovery whilst engaged in the fulfilment of their public duties, might be prejudicial to the public interest:

"AND WHEREAS, also *in such cases of discovery by private citizens, they should be protected in their said rights by the Federal Government; therefore, be it enacted, &c.*"

The conceptions in italics clearly show that the propositions contrary to those they involve, are those generally received, and for this reason it was the pretension of the claimants to destroy them by a legislative act sanctioned expressly for the case.

It is idle to say that such insane principles, as those set down in the clauses of the project, could be sanctioned by the Congress of the Union. They were rejected.

It has been demonstrated that the claimant's clandestine expedition from the United States, not having discovered Isla de Aves, nor having taken possession of the same by an express commission from the nation, could not acquire a title of property worthy of respect by other nations, and therefore lack the right to legitimate any protection on the part of the Federal Government.

PROPOSITION FIFTH.

THE GOVERNMENT OF THE UNITED STATES HAS RECOGNIZED THE SOVEREIGNTY OF VENEZUELA OVER ISLA DE AVES.—Nothing more eloquent than the facts relating to this point which have been set forth in chronological order.

It follows, therefore, that the Legation of the United States then regarded Isla de Aves as the property of Venezuela, so as to ask for the usufruct thereof in favor of the Wallace assignees, and now looks upon it as the property of American citizens, in order to support and confirm the present claim for indemnification.

Such is the delicate, not to say false position in which the Government of the United

States has been placed by the acts of Mr, Eames. It is worth while to examine how he has attempted to extricate himself from the dilemma.

It is important to bear in mind that in December, 1854, occurred the act originating the present controversy, and also that the Government of Venezuela leased the island to Mr. Wallace. The Pickrell claim originated in September, 1855.

Well then Mr. Eames, in his note of March 31, 1857, says to Señor Gutierrez:

"Both the Government of the United States and the undersigned distinctly and affirmatively refused all manner of sanction to that contract, in so far as it related to the Island of Aves in question; and this refusal of all such sanction was officially made known to the Government of Venezuela, by the undersigned, in his immediate notification to the Government of Venezuela in the month of March, 1855, of the claim of these claimants for full indemnification for their unlawful expulsion, in consequence of that contract from the Island of Aves."

The first conception in the preceding paragraph seeks to establish that it belonged to Mr. Eames to sanction the Wallace contract. Such intervention, indeed, was altogether inconsistent with the nature of the case from the outset.

As to the immediate notification, the Government of Venezuela replied in its note of 31st October ultimo, as follows:

"It is not correct that Mr. Eames has clearly and affirmatively refused to sanction the contract in so far as it relates to Isla de Aves, although in 1855 he alluded, while in *conversation* with the Seceretary of Foreign Affairs, Señor Aranda, to the claim which some individuals residing thereon *endeavored* to establish."

This conversation took place about the latter part of March, 1855, and the same official note from Mr. Eames to Mr. Marcy, April 26, 1855—the first upon the subject—goes to show that the aforesaid conference was not intended solely, *distinctly and affirmatively to refuse the sanction of the Wallace contract, but to acquire data for officially grounding the Shelton claim.*

"I had learned most of these facts when, in the last days of last month (March,) shortly after the receipt of your instruction, I brought the matter to the attention of this Government. I prefered *to do this first in conversation, for I had heard something to the effect that the Americans on the island had, upon the arrival of the Venelan vessels there, signed a contract, &c.*

"I therefore, in a personal interview, placed before the Minister of Foreign Relations, as distinctly as possible the main facts of the case, as presented in your instruction and the accompanying paper, expressing my astonishment at the course pursued by Venezuela, and stating my expectation that the wrong would be at once recognized and repaired."

"In reply the Minister at once and very confidently denied that any wrong had been intended or done, and that any reparation could be properly claimed. He insisted, &c."

"I expressed strongly my dissent from this opinion, &c.

"I told him *I was aware of the Wallis* (Wallace) *contract*, and also aware that Venezuela had inserted a clause plainly showing a consciousness that the island was not hers, by refusing to guaranty the privilege she conceded; (*Mr. Eames seems to forget the pretensions of Holland, of which he speaks in this same note.*) I added . . . He rejoined . . . I said, as we parted, that I very much regretted to find so wide a difference of opinions between us upon a matter which, as it stood before me, appeared so serious. But I felt, as I left him, well assured *that, anticipating a discussion in writing*, he considered he had an impregnable case against the claim, and was reserving his fire.

"*Soon afterwards*, and while I was still *seeking to ascertain the exact nature of admissions* which I should have to encounter in prosecuting the reclamations of the claimants, there was put into my hand, by a merchant here, a paper which purported to be a copy of an agreement entered into and signed at the Island of Aves, &c."

After the month of April, 1855, up to September of the same year, Mr. Eames made no exertion whatever, either verbally or in writing, about the claim now before the Government of Venezuela, as shown by the following paragraph extracted from the aforesaid note which Mr. Eames addressed to Señor Gutierrez, March 31st, 1857.

"These two notes of the 24th of September, 1855, (*Memorandum,*) and of the 8th of March, 1855, (*in opposition to the claim of Holland,*) were repeatedly referred to by the undersigned in his note of the 20th of December last, and such having been from the first, and up to the present time, the recorded and steadily maintained position of the undersigned and of the Government of the United States as to the rights and claims of the present claimants, &c."

It follows, therefore, that during the first seven months elapsed after the armed occupation of Isla de Aves by Venezuela, Mr. Eames, having in view the introduction of the Shelton claim, made no kind of reservation, either verbally or in writing, concerning the Wallace contract.

In September, 1855, arose the claim of Pickrell, the agent for the Wallace assignees. It is now incumbent on the Government of Venezuela to show that:

☞ The American Minister, on the occasion referred to, did not, as he has since alleged, *except* Isla de Aves from the claim which he endorsed, and therefore did acknowledge the sovereignty of Venezuela over said island.

Mr. Eames has attempted to prove the express exception by the following words of his Memorandum, dated September 24th, 1855:

"After this preliminary reference, and having previously presented to his Excellency the agent of the company, the undersigned proceeded officially to make known to his Excellency, what he had previously declared to the Minister of his Excellency's Government, that in rendering his good offices in aid of the purposes of the agent of the company, to secure their rights as the assignees of the Wallace contract, the undersigned was emphatically instructed to forbear from saying or doing anything which could in the slightest degree affect or impair the claim against the Venezuelan Government for full reparation on the part of those Americans citizens whom Venezuela had found in the possession of the Aves Island in December last. The undersigned explained therefore, fully and clearly to his Excellency, that all which he might say or do in aid of the agent of the company, must be understood with this express reservation: *that the Aves claim was a wholly separate matter in no way to be compromised or affected by any arrangement which might be made in respect to the rights under the Wallace contract, or by any aid which the undersigned might render in bringing about such an arrangement.*"

Substantially what do those words mean? "I countenance the Pickrell claim, protesting that I do not renounce the right to support afterwards the Shelton claim." Such protest or reservation far from excepting Isla de Aves, far from making both claims consistent, show a deliberate purpose to slight the conflict involved by both; and therefore does not relieve the Government of the United States from the delicate position in which it has been placed by its exacting, in favor of certain American citizens, compliance with a contract which presupposes Venezuela as the sovereign over Isla de Aves, and by afterwards refusing to acknowledge the same sovereignty in order to demand indemnification in favor of other American citizens.

Mr. Eames further states in this note of the 31st of March, that the Pickrell contract "omitted all mention of the Aves in the article guarantying the usufruct of the guano islands of the Republic to the assignees of that contract, and afterwards, in another article, specified the Aves apparently with the object of relieving Venezuela from liability to those assignees, in the event that her possession and use of it, for her own profit, should in view of this claim, or for any other reason, terminate."

This allegation is *contraproducentem*, that is, contrary to what it is designed to prove. The demonstration is very easy. What really occurred in the Pickrell contract was that although Isla de Aves was not specified in article 1st, it being comprised in the other guano islands of the Republic, it was notwithstanding distinctly mentioned in article 5th, in order to relieve Venezuela from any liability to the Philadelphia Company, in the eventual case of a cession in any arrangements with Holland. Mr. Eames alleges that the reservation had in view not the claim of Holland, but that of Shelton, which he had then *in contemplation.* So then, such forced conjecture involves the same object as the true cause of the reservation: it supposes, likewise, the including of Isla de Aves in the Pickrell contract, and therefore this admission, through the interference of the American Legation, implies the recognition of Venezuela's sovereignty over the island.

In order to obviate such a conflict, Mr. Eames, in September, 1855, had at his command two alternatives equally reasonable, but also equally unadapted, owing to the peculiar circumstances in which he found himself with regard to the opposing claimants.

☞One was: to support the Pickrell claim to *the express exclusion of Isla de Aves.*

But Mr. Eames could not act in such a manner, for the powerful reason that the very nature of the Philadelphia enterprise made *the exception impossible.* The fact has been above established, that the Pickrell protest referred specially to the guano from Isla de Aves. If Mr. Eames had attempted to except it at the time, Mr. Pickrell would not have consented to it, because the labors of the company being confined to Isla de Aves, the claim would have proved of no effectual benefit. This is confirmed by the fact of the Philadelphia Company having resumed the exportation of guano from Isla de Aves, as soon as Mr. Pickrell renewed the Wallace contract.

☞The other was: to accumulate the two claims, so as afterwards to dispose of them at the will of the parties with opposing rights.

So it was proposed by his Excellency, the President of Venezuela, in the conference alluded to in Mr. Eames' Memorandum, 24th September; but the United States Legation refused to adopt the measure.

"In reply to a remark from his Excellency, expressing his preference that the claim in regard to the previous occupation of the Aves Island should, if possible, be disposed of in any arrangement which might be made with the agent of the company, the undersigned answered, as he had before answered to his Excellency's Minister upon the same point, *that any such disposition of the Aves claim was wholly impossible*, not only by reason of the entirely distinct character of the two subjects, and of the duty of the undersigned to treat them separately, but also by reason of the fact that the undersigned *was not yet fully in possession of all the information requisite* for the due adjustment of the Aves claim."

What is, however, most strange in the incidental question bearing upon the fact of Mr. Eames excepting or not Isla de Aves in the Pickrell contract of 29th September, it is that the inclusion is proved by the confession of Mr. Eames himself in his note of March 8, 1856, to Señor Gutierrez opposing the cession of Isla de Aves demanded by Holland.

"The undersigned, in this connexion, deems it his duty further to state that he has in his possesion a copy of a contract entered into on the 29th of September last between the Government of Venezuela and John F. Pickrell, a citizen of the United States, conveying to the said contractor and his associates certain exclusive privileges in the guano islands of Venezuela, in which contract *the undersigned perceives that the Island of Aves, in question, is specified* under certain conditions and stipulations therein set forth."

True it is that Mr. Eames in the same note, March 8, undoubtedly perceiving the force of such confession extorted from him by the truth of the fact, sought to invalidate it by these words: "The undersigned, in view of that reservation, now abstains from giving any manner of sanction to the insertion of the Aves Island in that contract."

But such declaration is of no use when contrasted with a fixed fact. The whole of the learned world agrees upon this maxim " *Protestatio contra factum nihil revelat.*" So that the proof is utterly useless when the fact protested against, cannot be supported under any other head than that of renunciation. Facts, says Mr. Troplong, must be stronger than vain words.

It follows, from what is above set forth in the premises, that Venezuela, as the possessor and owner of Isla de Aves, ceded her usufruct thereof to the American citizen, Mr. Wallace, in December 1854: that the United States Legation at Caracas, whether in March 1855, when officially informed of the claim being presented at Washington by Shelton and associates, or even afterwards, did not transmit to the Government of Venezuela any determination on the part of the American Cabinet objecting to the lessees of the guano islands of the Republic to continue in the enjoyment of the benefit of Isla de Aves, because of its being deemed the property of other American citizens; and that far from doing so, this very Legation strongly interfered on the Pickrell question, in order to retain the usufruct of the island for the Wallace assignees.

The Government of Venezuela, relying upon these facts, holds that her sovereignty over Isla de Aves has been recognized by the Government of the United States by acts of unequivocal significance, leaving no room whatsoever for further protest.

PROPOSITION SIXTH.

IRRESPONSIBILITY OF VENEZUELA.—This is a conclusion which naturally follows from the facts and reasonings already established.

1st. If Isla de Aves is the property of Venezuela, as has been proved by strong titles and acts of the complaining government itself, the American citizens by invading it in 1854, committed an act of filibusterism.

The fact of their being even the first to discover guano thereon, did not vest them with the right to make themselves masters of the *accessions*, which nobody can deny, belongs to the owner of the territory.

However, they acknowlege the fact of their having been found on the island in December, with vessels ready to load guano, and of their having previous to the above date, already extracted therefrom a considerable quantity of the article. So then Venezuela should have regarded them as pirates taken by surprise or *in flagrante delicto.*

Their peaceful expulsion, far from making it an act of violence to merit indemnification, is one of condescension and kindness which the United States ought undoubtedly to acknowledge.

2d. If Isla de Aves is not the property of Venezuela, it must needs belong to Holland, who claims it.

The acts exercised thereon by American citizens do not for this reason change their character. They are no less filibustering and piratical, the islet belonging to Venezuela, than they would be, were it the property of Holland. As such, the Venezuelan navy had a right to expel them from the territory of a friendly nation.

On the supposition alluded to, the claimants have not the least right to demand indemnification from Venezuela, just as Walker and his followers could have no right to demand indemnification from Spain, if one of her Admirals had assumed the position of Commodore Paulding in the late events at Punta Arenas.

On the supposition under consideration, Venezuela would have violated the territory of Holland, and this nation would have been the one to resent the injury done ; but the pirates could not have acquired the right to demand indemnification from Venezuela, for the same reason that the United States will never award reparation to the invader of Nicaragua, notwithstanding it being officially established that a commander of the national navy *violated a foreign territory* in order to succeed in the capturing of the filibusters.

The present administration of the United States Government, which has assumed so strong a position on account of the Paulding-Walker affair, cannot fail to recognize the identity of the two cases. At least, it may be so presumed in view of the sound principles professed by the American press, which sustains the predominant policy of the ruling administration. We have only to substitute in the present international claim alluded to, the agents of the case, in order to manifest the justice of Venezuela, sustained by the Committee of Foreign Relations of the Senate, and by the "Washington Union" of January 31.

" 'The South' is compelled to dissent from both the premises and the conclusion of the able report of Mr. Mason of the Senate Committee of Foreign Relations in the Paulding-Walker case. 'The South,' after stating the position of the committee that the affair of the arrest (*expulsion*) only concerns the Government of the United States and the Government of Nicaragua (*the Government of Venezuela, and the Government of Holland*) exclaims with some enthusiasm : "*What ! is not reparation due the individuals who are the victims of an act of legal violence and unwarrantable usurpation ?* "The South' (*the attorney of the claimants*) is sufficiently conversant with the principles of law, to understand that a party detected in the violation of statutes may not invoke the civil arm of government to put him right. If Gen. Walker (*Shelton party*) set on foot a military (*filibuster*) expedition against the State of Nicaragua, (*the Dutch Isla de Aves,*) in contempt of our laws, it would be a monstrous perversion of well defined legal practice to yield to his demands of restitution and redress. If the expedition referred to left our shores illegally, Gen. Walker and his men in connexion therewith, (*the invaders of Isla de Aves,*) can never be treated as citizens having the right to claim the protection of the government. They are *tainted* with wrong. Nor can we agree with "The South" (*attorney of the claimants*) that natural sovereignty is such an unappeasable organ, as to be incapable of determining the extent of its own wrongs, and of deciding upon the manner of their redress. If the sovereignty of Nicaragua (*Holland*) has been violated by us (*Venezuela,*) we insist that Nicaragua (*Holland*) shall at least have the right to say how much, if any, she is injured, and what will satisfy her. We go so far as to maintain, in opposition to "The South,' that it is clearly the right of any nation to consent to the military occupation of its soil by another, &c."

3d. Finally, if Isla de Aves was *derelict* in July, 1854, Venezuela, by occupying it, has not incurred any liability towards the American citizens whom she found there in December of the same year.

International law authorized Venezuela to do so, as has been shown above.

Besides, the American claimants themselves freely consented to the occupation by Venezuela in the following document:

"*Domingo Diaz, captain of a ship-of-war, and second chief of the Venezuelan navy, and commissioned by the supreme government of the Republic to watch the desert Antilles that belong to it in the Carribean sea, has agreed, subject to the approbation of my government, that Messrs. Charles H. Lang, (agent of the company of " Lang & Delano, of Boston,) and Nathan P. Gibbs, (agent of that of Sampson, Tappan & P. S. Shelton, also of Boston,) whom I have found extracting guano from this island, may :*

" 1. *Continue to load the vessels that are actually taking in cargo.*

" 2. *They may continue to load until the arrival of the company with whom the government has entered into contracts, or until the arrival of the approbation, or disapprobation of the supreme government.*

" 3. *And we, Charles H. Lang and Nathan P. Gibbs, engage to lend the aid that the garrison of the island may require.*

" 4. *And to that effect we place our pieces of artillery and armament at the orders and under the Venezuelan flag, to which the island belongs ; and,*

" 5. *I, Diaz, second chief of the Venezuelan navy, do order the commanders of men-of-war cruising in the Antilles to respect the concession until the supreme government may dispose otherwise.*

"NATHAN P. GIBBS.
"CHARLES H. LANG,
" *Agent for Lang & Delano, Boston.*
"DOMINGO DIAZ.

" Island of Aves, [*to windward,*]
" *December* 13, 1854."

It now becomes proper to make mention of this incident, which proves the last assertion. As is already apparent, however favorable for Venezuela, her Government has not required it for the justification of her conduct in the claim.

The agent for the two Boston Houses acknowledged, in the above quoted document, the legitimacy of Venezuela's authority over Isla de Aves. The moment they thought of a lucrative claim upon that Republic, the first thing to which they ought to have called the attention of their government, if they had actually been wronged, or deceived, in the act in question, was the existence of the permit of December 13th. So remarkable an incident could not have been overlooked, through forgetfulness, in a claim, the justice of which depended precisely upon the value that might be attached to that document.

However, it will be seen that Shelton and associates did not think of the exception of fraud and violence, until the American Legation found itself unexpectedly stopped in its proceedings by the permit of December 13th, 1854.

The claimants laid the case before the Government of the United States, January 15th, 1855, without mentioning the incident operating against them. This is the manner in which it was discovered by Mr. Eames, and the impression it made on him. The following are paragraphs from his note to Mr. Marcy, dated at Caracas, April 26, 1855, in which he goes on to relate what had occurred after his interview with the Secretary of Foreign Relations, about the latter part of March, as has been stated above :

" Soon afterwards, and while I was still seeking to ascertain the exact nature of the admission, which I should have to encounter in prosecuting the reclamation of the claimants, there was put in my hands, by a merchant here, a paper which purported to be a copy of an agreement entered into and signed at the Island of Aves on the 13th of December last. . . . . Upon comparing this paper with the documents accompanying your instruction, which purported to invoke your interposition upon a full narration of the very events in which this paper forms so material a portion, the first inclination of my mind was either to doubt its genuineness, or the accuracy of the copy on my hands. I therefore took an early opportunity to have another interview with Mr. Aranda, in which I informed him that I had what purported to be a copy of one of the papers in the case, which, at this stage of business, I wished to compare with the original. He at once assented, though he could not understand how a copy should have got out, and at a subsequent day, placed the papers in my hands for examination. I found the original there—to all appearance an authentic paper—and upon comparison, my copy proved to be exact. I then asked Mr. Aranda if he was satisfied of the genuineness of the original, and he replied that there could not be a doubt of it.

"With these facts before me, *I find myself unable to resist the conviction that the case of the claimants is clothed by this paper with a character very different from that in which they brought it to your notice, and upon which your instruction was framed.* If the case was one of a conflicting claim between the two governments, to the eminent domain of the Aves, this agreement I should consider of no force whatever. But the case being a reclamation of private citizens for indemnity and restoration, I cannot avoid the conclusion that the claimants themselves have, by this act of their agents, if left unexplained, greatly embarrassed their government in its successful prosecution. At all events, there can be no doubt that the agreement of the claimants is regarded by the Venezuelan Government as an effectual bar to any claim for indemnity by them or in their behalf.

"In this state of facts, I deem it proper to refer this new matter in the case to the Department, in order to learn the view which you take of its bearing upon the further prosecution of the claim. I am the more induced to adopt this course because, considering the date of this agreement, *I see no reason to doubt that it was known to the claimants when they presented their case to you on the 15th of January last, and I cannot understand what is their justification for not then bringing it to your attention, with whatever explanation of it might be in their power.* It is proper to add, however, that I have of course made no admission whatever to this government, as to the paper or the operation of it, and that when I receive your views of it, and of the case as affected by it, I shall be prepared to carry your instructions at once into effect."

When the claimants found themselves overwhelmed by a proof so decidedly against them, they then conceived the plan of making it void by launching a gross imputation upon an unblemished and honorable Venezuelan chieftain. They have not dared to deny their own signatures; they have only endeavored to make believe that force and fraud were used for the purpose of obtaining their acquiescence.

Force and fraud! Two actions which never go together, because the nature of each by itself excludes the other. The claimants, however, maintain that force and fraud intervened in the permit in question.

It is important to bear in mind the two versions suggested by the above mentioned incident.

The version of the Venezuelan Government is:

That Colonel Diaz, on the 13th of December, landed in Isla de Aves without any opposition, either by words or deeds on the part of the American citizens there found; that at their request and entreaty the permit referred to was conceded; and that by various attentions shown the Venezuelans, did the Americans appear to be pleased and obliged by the act of compliance of the Venezuelan Commissioner.

The claimants' version supported by the United States Legation at Caracas is:

That they did *verbally* oppose the occupation of the Island by Venezuela: that, *ia fact*, they did not do it, although with a superior force to that effect, with the view of avoiding extremities: and that the two agents for the Boston Houses signed the document as well to prevent the use of force, as because of their ignorance that the permit in Spanish contained the recognition of Venezuela's title over the Isla de Aves.

The party for Shelton and associates has endeavored to prove his allegation, summoning various witnesses connected with the two Isla de Aves expeditions, some to declare before a Justice of the Peace in Boston, and others before a Notary public in New York.

The Government of Venezuela has repelled the false allegation by declarations from the commanders and officers who occupied the island on the 13th of December, 1854; all of which were taken at the office of the Secretary of War, in the presence of Mr Sandford, Shelton's agent at Caracas.

Which of the two versions is the true one? If the contending governments recognized one superior judge to weigh the proofs adduced by both parties, that of Venezuela would unquestionably be sustained by the following reasons, which, being the principal ones, are drawn from the whole of the testimony.

There was no fraud, 1st, because Mr. Lang, one of the two American agents, is very well acquainted with the Spanish language; 2d, because the permit, before Mr. Gibbs, the other agent, had signed it, was interpreted for him by Lang himself and by Commander Cotarro, of the Venezuela navy.

There was no violence, 1st, because the document was signed when there were but three Venezuelan officers on shore; 2d, because even had the whole of the detachment and crew on board the schooner landed, the numerical superiority on the filibuster's side made fear impossible, even in men not so strong and resolute as they represented themselves in their declarations; and 3d, because these very invaders themselves, although obliged to prove such imaginary violence, have not ventured to mention any act of compulsion, death, wounds, or even blows.

The Superior Judge, supposed in the case, would have seen, as already stated, that fraud and violence are actions excluding each other, from their very nature; that the very conduct of the American signers, such as is represented by their own declarations, before the act, during the act, and after the act of the permit, compels common sense to reject the allegation; and he must finally have seen that the proof, proceeding from a written document against the signers thereof, is always conclusive, since by their own allegations, no legislation could invalidate it.

Yet Venezuela and the United States, equally independent, equally sovereign, do not recognize any Superior Judge impartially to weigh the proofs adduced. It belongs, therefore, to their respective governments to fulfil this delicate function, guided only by principles of justice.

The Government of Venezuela, with a perfect knowledge of the case, has advanced its views on the question; they are very evident; they have herein been set forth, and clear it is, that it could not be possible to enunciate them with stronger foundation.

The Government of the United States must now, in its turn, express its opinion. Presided over as it is by a theoretically and practically just administration, Venezuela has a right to expect from it a disregard for the alleged exception of fraud and violence, not only in consideration of the reasons already given, but also because in the obtaining of the testimony presented by the claimants, there have been omitted all the tutelar formalities to ensure credibility of the witnesses, as those connected with the case have never been brought to trial by judicial proceedings, nor have in their favor the guarantee of public examination.

All these guarantees were obtained by the evidence which the Government of the United States presented to Great Britain in the recent question about recruiting; and yet, when Lord Clarendon, in the name of his government, disregarded it on the ground of not being satisfactory, the Secretary of State, Mr. Marcy, did not arrogate to himself the right to judge alone and on his own authority of the value of the testi mony presented, notwithstanding its having been obtained in a public, formal trial and corroborated with very important documents; but thought himself in duty bound to declare in his note of 13th of October, 1855, to the American Plenipotentiary in London, that:

"Should her Britanic Majesty's Government see fit to disclose any specific objection to the *mode* by which the evidence has been obtained, or attempt in any other way to impeach it, *this government will then feel called on to vindicate its course, and show its ability to sustain its charges by evidence to which no just exception can be taken.*"

How could then the Government of Venezuela expect, in the controverted case, that the United States, disregarding such sacred forms, should deliberately sustain extrajudicial declarations of interested witnesses, too suspicious to the effect of exacting undue indemnification from a whole nation? Such a proceeding would present a repugnant contrast with that required by the ordinary course of the Union and of all other civilized nations, to condemn a single individual in a trial involving comparatively insignificant pecuniary interests.

In an international question, therefore, in which much more transcendental interests are concerned, the Government of the United States will require, for the purpose of its convictions, what it is known is required in weighing the proofs of contradictory testimony: not only the preponderance of proofs, so that the one against the defendant will palpably exceed the one in his favor, but the full and satisfactory evidence, that is, such a degree of proof as will leave no reasonable doubt with regard to truth.

This evidence, thus qualified, is what the claimants have not presented, so as to destroy the value of the permit of December 13th, and consequently even in the denied admission of Isla de Aves, being deemed *derelict*, there would be no ground left for the required liability of Venezuela.

The above statement of the justification of Venezuela would not be complete, did it not further evidence that Mr. Eames had erroneously informed the cabinet of Washington that the cabinet of Caracas had wilfully retarded the consideration of this affair, whereas, by the official acts of both cabinets, quite the contrary is shown.

In March 1855, Mr. Eames received from Mr. Marcy the first official note on the subject. In the same month, and in April following, he procured two interviews with the Secretary of Foreign Relations, for the purpose of obtaining information. Afterwards, he had occasion *to mention the intended claim* on the Pickrell question, (September, 1855,) and on that of Holland (March, 1856). The last declarations which the claimants tried when they thought of annulling the permit of 13th December, were rendered in April, 1856. This last incident shows that Mr. Eames could not have introduced the claim into the cabinet of Caracas before the 20th of December, 1856.

If, as it has been pretended, the claim was presented in the *conversation* of March, 1855, without any documentary evidence to sustain it, it is now about three years since it was initiated; but even in such an inadmissible case, the *discussion* could only have taken place on the 20th December, 1856, when Mr. Eames presented his written demand. All the time, therefore, that the protected citizens required for obtaining their proofs against the permit of the 15th December, is attributed to procrastination on the part of Venezuela.

In one way or the other, the truth is, that the *discussion* did not commence until the 20th December, 1856. The Government of Venezuela contested the claim, repudiating it in a note of the 27th February, 1857. On the 31st March, Mr. Eames insisted in an extensive note, accompanied with the evidence of the claimants; and without allowing time for the examination thereof, arrogated to himself the right of terminating the discussion, scarcely yet opened between two equal States that maintain and cultivate the most friendly relations with each other.

And what was his subsequent course of procedure? He still persists in denying to Venezuela the necessary time to collect such evidence in the case, as was required to oppose that presented by Shelton and his associates. He pays no attention to the official citation served on him for the taking thereof, pretending thereby, it may be presumed, to put out of question those facts of fraud and violence which for the first time opposed the permit of December 13th; and finally, having obtained permission from his government to return to his country, he ostentatiously demanded his passports, leaving it to be inferred, as the result of the pending question, and as placing the relations of the two countries *in a state full of perils.*

The Government of Venezuela, nevertheless, firm in its purpose to maintain its dignity, did not abandon its unquestionable right. Although engaged at the time with the sessions of Congress, and occupied by important public business, it lost no time in collecting the mass of facts that were necessary to answer directly to the cabinet of Washington, as was done in its reasonable note of October 31st ultimo, and to fix the solution of the question at this capital, sending to that effect the undersigned Envoy Extraordinary and Minister Plenipotentiary

M. DE BRICEÑO.

WASHINGTON CITY, *March* 1, 1858.

www.ingramcontent.com/pod-product-compliance
Lightning Source LLC
LaVergne TN
LVHW011141110826
845150LV00008B/2449

* 9 7 8 1 4 1 8 1 9 3 0 7 2 *